Letters to Minnehaha Creek

Letters to Minnehaha Creek

Victoria Lin

Letters to Minnehaha Creek
Copyright © 2020 Victoria Lin
All Rights Reserved
Published by Unsolicited Press
Printed in the United States of America.
First Edition.

No part of this book may be used or reproduced in any manner whatsoever without written permission except in the case of brief quotations embodied in critical articles or reviews.

Attention schools and businesses: for discounted copies on large orders, please contact the publisher directly.

For information contact:
Unsolicited Press
Portland, Oregon
www.unsolicitedpress.com
orders@unsolicitedpress.com
619-354-8005

Cover Design: Lucy Comer
Editor: Rachel Warren
Editor: S.R. Stewart

ISBN: 978-1-950730-43-8

I thank my dear friend, Dorothy, for ten years of an extraordinary friendship, and my mentor Katrina for helping me find a way to write through my grief after Dorothy's death. I thank the staff at Unsolicted Press for their wise and thoughtful attention to these poems.

I thank my husband and children for accommodating my inability to cook without setting off the fire alarm and my difficulty with remembering rules to common games, like *Uno*, because I am too busy thinking about poetry.

I thank my writers' group at Solomon's Porch, comprised of those who support my work and offer endless encouragement to keep writing. I thank Brent and Renea for being the most reassuringly adept, short-notice readers to support me as I prepared to let these poems go out into the world.

I thank everyone who has ever read or listened to something I have written.

Table of Contents

Walking to Meet Dorothy   9
Alone   10

Fall   13
   Letters to Minnehaha Creek: Prelude   14
   Letters to Minnehaha Creek: I   15
   Letters to Minnehaha Creek: II   19
   Letters to Minnehaha Creek: III   21
   Letters to Minnehaha Creek: IV   25
   Letters to Minnehaha Creek: V   28
   Letters to Minnehaha Creek: VI   29
   Letters to Minnehaha Creek: VII   33
   Lost   38

Winter   41
   Letters to Minnehaha Creek: VIII   42
   Letters to Minnehaha Creek: IX   45
   Letters to Minnehaha Creek: X   48
   Letters to Minnehaha Creek: XI   51
   Letters to Minnehaha Creek: XII   54

Letters to Minnehaha Creek: XIII	57
Letters to Minnehaha Creek: XIV	60
Letters to Minnehaha Creek: XV	63
Tracking	66
Landscape with Primary Colors	67
Spring	69
Letters to Minnehaha Creek: XVI	70
Letters to Minnehaha Creek: XVII	73
Letters to Minnehaha Creek: XVIII	76
Letters to Minnehaha Creek: XIX	78
Letters to Minnehaha Creek: XX.	81
Letters to Minnehaha Creek: XXI.	83
The Life of Yard Ornaments	86
Summer	87
Letters from Minnehaha Creek: I	88
Letters from Minnehaha Creek: II	89
Letters from Minnehaha Creek: III	90
Afterward	91

Walking to Meet Dorothy

I cannot see the tumors in her lungs
living silently like cauliflower
florets. I cannot see the drug that slows
the small-cell growth, even
those in her curly, steel-colored hair.

But she is waving at the bottom
of the hill bordered by oaks,
their yellow leaves hanging
on as the frost plans to strip
the branches bare to the bark.

Alone

I want to do it again —
give Dorothy the last sponge bath, be more
careful with her sore shoulder

this time. I would not chatter
about when the nurse washed
my hair after bunion surgery.

I would ask her about school
at the convent, her former desire to be a saint.
She would tell me about her family farm

and when she accidentally melted the bottoms
of her pink slippers onto the wood stove.
I would slowly rinse the soap, listening,

ask her to tell me about the day
she knew she was on her own. She stood
at the bottom of a steep,

steep hill, thick, slick
with ice. After a long, thoughtful pause,
she accepted that no one

would rescue her.
I want to ask her how she
made her way up.

Fall

Letters to Minnehaha Creek: Prelude

I am coming to you now.
When Dorothy was alive, I did not

think of you as much more
than the scenery

framing our friendship. She
noticed when you were low

or high or altered.
Do you notice

that I am alone?
Do you save anything?

Do you keep some
of the world in your watery

heart? Do you remember her?

Letters to Minnehaha Creek: I

Do you want more than you have?
I will bring you everything I can:

The wood ducks that have not
yet left Powderhorn Park.

Peppermint tea at Mayday Café
and the pink hay-bale house

still unfinished. Falling leaves
you have and the trees

along your path. I will bring you
whatever you want. The graveyard,

all those dancing bones are yours.
The Tudor with the barking dogs.

The father telling his child,
Stop worrying about that.

The tarp over Seven Star
Missionary Baptist Church,

the plastic strip of flags glistening
as ice in the sun. I cannot bring

the names of the trees and birds.
She knew them, but I only remember

her name.
Dorothy.

The American flag I can bring you,
the strollers and foreclosure signs.

The bird baths, the sedum, and mums still blooming.
Carved pumpkins, as many as you want,

and the Kleenex ghosts suspended
on wire by the sidewalk.

There is no one else
waiting for what I have.

I do this for her memory.
She would say, *Do it for yourself.*

Here is the smell of burning bread,
the softness of the pussy willow shrub.

Here is the weight
of her absence.

You saunter,
low and heavy with leaves.

The echo of cars on the parkway will not
stop you. Nor will heavy machinery

repairing the road or the wind
and anticipation of snow.

The baptism of all these leaves
will not make you quit. The cancer

had its way with her too. It kept
moving until she stopped. But

the weight of my loss will not stop you.
You move as you were meant to move.

How far would I go
if I moved like you?

She brought extra gloves in winter
and reading glasses to see

my poems. She brought
plastic bags to sit on wet ground.

The hawthorn berries bring everything.
Hanging on shrubs,

skin pitted, insides dry. Red
remains for birds to pluck one by one.

The seeds bring promises that sleep.

Letters to Minnehaha Creek: II

Down Aldrich Avenue,
tidy yards devoid of ornaments.

If Dorothy were here, we would discuss
home owners with time to do the work

or money to pay someone else
to rake leaves, fill the eco bags,

line them along the sidewalk.
We would decide to like

our neighborhood better with its purple
houses and hoses left out all winter.

I shimmy past the sign that says,
Path closed. Danger.

There is no ice yet.
Gray steps, set below

the swish, swish
of cars passing over

the bridge and the rumble
of planes far above.

A woman says, *Look
for raccoons in the holes.*

Wait and watch.
Nothing.

Is it possible to observe
what we do not understand?

I once thought I would walk
more slowly without Dorothy. But

I keep the same pace now.
Does it feel like work

to you, adapting constantly?
Orange and red graffiti borders

the arch under the bridge. I understand it
as well as the speech of concrete.

A pair of mallards swim
by as I find my way up the stairs.

A female cardinal
in scalloped flight moves

across the sky alone, surprised
at times her partner is gone.

I am tempted to shout to her.
I want company

on the long way home.
The red bell

maintains the silence.

Letters to Minnehaha Creek: III

The pound of pavement pulses up
through feet, ankles, and knees.

My hips and gut shake.
My brain sloshes in its cage.

Vibration of concrete tells you
I come. I am heavy with my own water.

Even the Boy Scout wreaths and their red bows
rattle in the graveyard.

I found Dorothy's favorite garden.
We would hang over

the picket fence to enjoy
it like a painting in a gallery.

Raised beds, astilbe,
hostas, and creeping charlie

sprawl. Echinacea
and the irises she loved.

Wooden boxes frame the dirt,
define the once wild space.

Her last year, she only planted
annuals. Did not replace

her broken clock.
The weight of wild time rules.

A man at his canvas paints the bridge, the trees,
and you. Not the dogs, the cars, or me.

We are outside his frame.
He adds more and more green,

leans closer, breathes in sync
with his canvas to see what he needs.

The breeze may blow you back.
It may vibrate my page.

I cannot have you
as you were before. Now I write

with the alphabet of grief.
I give you my hand. Your water,

heavy paint on my autumn canvas.

Letters to Minnehaha Creek: IV

Pass the morass
of Seagram's boxes,

the red door of Powderhorn
Park Neighborhood Association.

Pass the squirrels
hiding acorns

in the knots of bare branches.
Pass absence.

How many miles
have you traveled? We walked

five thousand on this webbed concrete.
Pass the chimes, and the plants

pressed against the windows,
looking for the sun.

The *Southside Pride* paper waits
on the steps of the empty

condo. Cut through McRae Park,
pass the empty hockey rink,

the empty wading pool, the playground,
the navy sweatshirt hanging on the bush.

Forty-two crows in the soccer field
have a lot to say about where

to go. Find a way through
their moving maze.

Pass the black chokeberries,
amongst the orange leaves, plump

as if impervious to the frost, waiting
for birds to offer passage to fertile land.

An old branch the color of dirt raises
its amputated limbs to the sky.

You chatter quickly over the rocks.
The chicken wire holds me back.

Today you are a girl at her
birthday party. Bare feet

guide you through the rocks. New blue
gingham dress, arms outstretched to the future,

green sash trailing miles and miles behind.
The tall yellow grass stands in awe

with the presence of mind to drink deeply.

Letters to Minnehaha Creek: V

Brown-needle and brown-leaf
rugs woven over grass.

The wood ducks,
gone until spring. I pick up

a handful of red maple leaves
as though I will mail them to Dorothy.

The weeping willow on the island
still holds its curled green leaves.

Does it know the distant sun will watch
them fade to brown and fall to the ground?

I close my eyes to see
your future flow.

Can you feel your rhythm
changing? Do you

dream of the freeze?

Letters to Minnehaha Creek: VI

Elm with orange ring
comes down.

Seven branches gone.
Seven more to go.

Truck blocks the whole street.
Grinding saw and cracking branches

in lieu of an elegy. There should
be a preacher to say a few

words, at least. We could pay
our respects, stand on the curved

porch of this little yellow house,
eat cold cuts and potato salad.

Dorothy said all Minneapolis
streets were once shady

under a canopy of elms. But one
disease knocked them all down

easily. Disappointed by the books
in the cancer library that focused

on keeping one's looks, Dorothy wrote
essays about living toward death.

I inhale the smell of a freshly cut lawn.
The roots of a fallen tree

witness your journey—damp
soil and grass clinging to make dreadlocks.

A dozen small oaks
uprooted with the fall

of this massive body.
I know you cannot do

anything differently
as you witness

their death. Dried dirt sighs
on the leaves at my feet.

Four months ago, a tornado
touched down on this block,

shredded the houses, roof
after roof being repaired.

Ropes attached to men
jutting out at odd angles,

shouting in Spanish, forming v's
with the roofline, swaying side to side

like an immigration elegy.
Fake red roses tucked

in a chain-link fence,
yellow ribbon tied around

thick oak, pictures of soldiers
killed in action taped to the trunk.

Should I build an altar
to hold my sorrow?

If God made the world in seven days,
why not dismantle grief in a week?

Plastic rainbow pinwheels spin.
The ant crawls into my notebook,

again. Now the rush
of engines reminds me to hurry

to pick up Mari. I am coming, daughter.

Letters to Minnehaha Creek: VII

I love the brown spheres
of the black-eyed Susans,

and the soft cylinders
of grass gone to seed,

these erect saints waiting for spring.
I love the memory of her

walking beside me.
She wanted a bench

for those she loved
to sit on when they visited

her grave. But she is not
buried yet, her ashes uninterred.

I love the sparrows clamoring
around the birdfeeder.

They peck at one another
until they get a beak

full and flutter
to a branch to eat.

I am the bird calling,
heep, heep, heep, heep.

I am the old oak, branches
shorn down to the trunk,

who once grew green.
I am a thin, new tree that leans

into the earth. I breathe, exposed
dirt, flexing itself, damp muscle.

I dare not drink you,
even though I am thirsty.

Tall, dry grass surrenders,
a dry stain of what was.

Single strands of spider
web shimmer. I wish

you could tell me
what the afterlife is like

for the dead. I walk across
the dry scar of your sandy belly

and place a blade of crabgrass
with a drop of water

in your wet remainder.

The Elm

I do not know when
it started. I refuse

to blame the beetles.
Nor do I blame

the fungus, dumbly
moving in my system.

The first two branches
died slowly, yellowing

to brown. You can see
the shape I was.

You cannot see the shape
I will become.

The cardinals build their nest,
too polite to mention

their branch is gone.
I hope to see the babies

hatch wet and blind.

Lost

> *Love means to learn to look at yourself*
> *The way one looks at distant things*
> *For you are only one thing among many.*
>
> — Czeslaw Milosz

I see the moon as it whispers
to sleep the tulips
and sparrows, so bats

may have their time
with transluscent wings. They call
to the spaces.

They hear where to fly.
The moon sees me —
accepts, knows, pulls

on the water of all bodies.
There is no stopping time.
The moon shifts

quick and wet, a river
that cannot be held
and drips from lips.

This is how I want
to live. Watch the moon.
It will reveal the way to go.

Winter

Letters to Minnehaha Creek: VIII

The sky sweeps its damp
hands over my hair.

I cannot wait to see what
the rain gives you. The cedar

fence, perfume for the worms.
The cars make music

with the puddles whispering,
luscious, luscious, luscious.

I am alive.
I can do anything. Wet baneberries

emit greenish-white light
as if they could glow in the dark.

I love these gray days when
the early Christmas lights glow.

These streets are mine.
My cells renew themselves

with every step. I pass
out confidence like Tic Tacs.

Pass through the arches of Phelps
Park marked with children's art,

frogs, dice, and a message
to Big T. Granny.

I pass through to another
self. There is enough room for

all of us in this wet air.
You are not a fat creek.

Wasn't the rain your
Thanksgiving feast? The hungry

sun covered in clouds cannot
feed its insatiable need.

My back rests against the metal
of the bridge. A squirrel

watches me out of one eye.
The cardinal watches me

out of another. Every time
I look they are somewhere new.

I think how differently
I would see with an eye

on each side of my head.

Letters to Minnehaha Creek: IX

Evidence of faith
is everywhere today.

Trees trained to grow two
dimensionally. A dumpster

full of wood, a mattress, lamp,
an upside-down chair.

Wheelbarrow with green stalks
yellowing. Smoke and noise

from a snow blower
when there is no snow.

The torn-up road and dirt
hole with the concrete cylinder

wait for new pipes.
What holds this together?

Bunches of orange
mountain ash berries hang

from the branches, pimply teenagers.
The woman and daughter

put up Christmas lights—
their bindis sparkle.

The holiday to honor the baby
of an adolescent virgin almost here.

I rest on the log of
the diseased tree

cut down. Ice is around
your edges. What holds you together?

The grave with roses
spelling mom,

bones and fur
of a dead squirrel,

geese feasting
in Powderhorn Lake,

tails gliding across the surface,
perhaps like reenactments of Peter

walking on water.

Letters to Minnehaha Creek: X

The wind pushes me to the alleys
where the garages offer shelter.

Empty paint cans and glass jars
line the fence. I loved

the alleys with Dorothy first.
The sunrooms and yards full of crap.

Alley days are like
sightseeing in another country.

Once we carried a chair
together all the way home.

In my basement now,
wires poke out of the seat.

Leaves blow along the concrete
with their own music. Once I played

on a stage with twenty
other pianists on grand pianos.

I can still hear it. But the music
of the world does not work

that way. I risk
attempting to order

its cacophony. A brand new
sign is on the driveway: *No Trespassing.*

I want to see the way you see,
with one direction to go,

fingers trailing in the mud,
bubble eyes on the sky.

I visit her garden for the first time
since the auction in her home.

Everything she owned put in piles
and sold. I hang over her fence.

Someone moved the flowering
kale and basil, rogue notes.

The tree she salvaged from the alley
is gone, a gaping hole

in its place. But I still have
the other tree she saved

staked on my boulevard,
oxygen breath,

invisible music.

Letters to Minnehaha Creek: XI

The yard sign quotes Paul
Wellstone, *Politics is what*

we create by what we work for,
what we hope for,

and what we dare to imagine.
Huge dog puppet rests

along the top of a station
wagon. Eyes, nose,

and tongue hovering
over the windshield.

Eight-foot Lucy statue carries mugs
of frothy root beer in the yard

next door. How much did it cost?
The last two years, Dorothy's drugs

 cost hundreds of dollars a month. She
was not sure it was fair to those

who live and die without enough.
But she still took the drugs, giving

us all more time to be alive
with her. The ornery old man

angrily rakes his leaves
watching his dog come over to me

out of the corner of his eye.
He yells, *Come here Charlie.*

Small branchy oak trees
surround the large trunk of the source.

I am glad for their company.
So many have lost

more than me. This is my palette:
grays, greens, browns,

a handful
of red lingonberries.

The sun hops off your surface,
leaves behind this half-moon.

Imagine freeing the stuffed animals
in the laundry basket who press

against the window and cry
Release us. Imagine all the Christmas

yard ornaments emigrate
to Canada — the bear

in the Santa hat leads the way.
The hand-painted station wagon

says, *Holy Jungle Burgers*
and *Non-stop Banjo.*

Let's drive it all over
the country, until the peace

signs create peace.

Letters to Minnehaha Creek: XII

Here is a small prairie on Fifth
Avenue. Grass and wildflowers

hold off concrete and buses
with their dried clothes.

I do not know
the name of this feeling —

is it longing or ecstasy?
I want to say to Dorothy,

*Here's something
we missed.*

She once said, *I am
 going to miss me.*

A honey-colored squirrel
glides by full of brown mystery.

Do you feel the pound
of copper pipes pressed

into your skin or the sparks
of the soldering iron?

Do you have a shield?
Oak tree roots dangle down

from the stump,
a dismembered hand

running its fingers
through your hair.

I cross the bridge under the diagonal
oak, stay on the path.

I would like to gather
you around me like a warm blanket

but you cannot chase the chill from my bones.
Can you feel your own mystery?

Snowflakes fall
intermittently. Past

Martin Luther King Park,
the Peterbilt truck

carries sod and a Bobcat
puts grass along the sound

barrier. I watch for a place
to warm up and rest.

El Paradiso Mexican
Restaurant is here, but

I do not have money.
I cross over the freeway,

the sole pedestrian walking over 35W,
eight lanes of fast machines

passing underneath.
I stop, press my forehead

against the chain-link fence,
submit to my slowness.

Something in me rushes away
at the speed of the cars—

lost before I name it.

Letters to Minnehaha Creek: XIII

Snow fills the slides
at Phelps Park. Abandoned

tires and flattened boxes
litter the sledding hill.

I glide through slush
the color of tree trunks.

I admit there are some
things I would not do

to have Dorothy here with me.
Gray, white, and black ice

capped with snow,
frozen like small mountains,

surrounding footprints
captured on uneven ground,

stilled movement on sidewalk.
Do you hold your breath,

a New Year's resolution,
hoping to move again, anywhere?

When Dorothy could
not breathe in the cold,

lungs filled with fluid,
we would loop around

the indoor Global Market.
Sometimes, she would rest

on a bench and say,
Keep going!

I walked back and forth
as she grinned, hair

falling out, maybe one hundred pounds.
When I ran

to hold the door
as we left,

she said, *I'm dying, but
I'm not diminished.*

As a three-year-old,
I insisted on going

out in three-degree
weather and did not come back

for too long. My mother
left my crying baby sister

to look for me.
Found me half-asleep,

breathing evenly
in a window well.

Sunlight bounces off
the ice. I go where

I cannot see.

Letters to Minnehaha Creek: XIV

I missed you from Hawaii
beside the bossy

ocean with its pull pull
pull. Instead all this

white white snow
we will not drown in.

Bicycle chained
to the fence—tire tracks

to the street mark
a trail, a memory.

I look up for the gargoyles
on the brick apartment,

wave to the woman
smoking on her balcony

in her bathrobe. The cold
scrapes at my thighs.

I remember when words made
and melted frost on our scarves.

Glass bottles clank
into the recycling truck.

The lanky man walks
just like Dorothy did, arms

swinging exclamation
points. His green coat

trailing away. I hear a baby wailing
for a block. What is your frozen cry?

Footprints and sled
tracks all over

the snow of your body.
I realize now, people,

rabbits, and birds use
you like a map

to get somewhere
else. I lean over

the bridge and weep.
The hollowed-out tree, only

half-gone, reaches toward the sky.
The ad for light fixtures

half-smothered in the snow.
I wore yellow to my Grandpa's

funeral. Hated everyone
who laughed. A month after

Dorothy's death, we made a celebration
in a room overlooking the Mississippi River.

Slides of her life on a big screen.
Hooked rugs and collages

she constructed bit
by bit hung on the walls,

like detours for grief.

Letters to Minnehaha Creek: XV

Ice under my feet
and music in my ears.

Ice skaters and boot skaters
on Powderhorn Lake.

My feet push
off the ground

and return with ease.
If only I could dance

with every branch that stretches
over the sky—understand

the space between notes.
Acorns fall in time

with dreams of death.
Will they remember

what they were when
they return? If I saw Dorothy,

would I know her? I compose
you with these leaning

grasses. These children
sledding on yellow,

green, and orange plastic. This rhythm,
this gift, to sit beside you,

a guest. Dorothy called her dying
a gift she did not want to give.

We played her honey-colored
grand piano for her

when she could not do it
anymore. Do you dance

with the melody of death?
Stuffed monkey leans on a tree, smiles

confidently as we join hands.
Sunlight dries sweat

around our necks.
We waltz. Shadows

circle us and lead.

Tracking

Mississippi ice broken
into angular shapes,

cubist sketch of itself.
Pepper runs and slides,

zips between
Carole and me,

paws not careful,
unlike us on our first walk

together. The metal
coils of our Yaktrax

marking the snow.
We are strange

animals who eat
sky and conversation—

itchy in our new fur.

Landscape with Primary Colors

I may see everything, but I have been blind
to the press of my breath on the atmosphere.
I am in a train I do not recognize.

The scenery is vivid—the colors only primary.
I imagine shades and variations that may not be
       there.
I may see everything, but I have been blind.

Before I arrive, I will bathe with Brent in candle
       light.
How much happiness can two bodies carry
while in a train I do not recognize?

The snow splashes backwards as the train climbs
from a valley with rock on both sides. Aware,
I may see everything, but I have been blind.

I know there are some things I will never find.
My cheek pressed to the window as I stare
out of a train I do not recognize.

My spirit did not flinch when I was a bride,
for years I only glimpsed it when it reared.
I may see everything, but I have been blind.
I am a train I do not recognize.

Spring

Letters to Minnehaha Creek: XVI

The snow melted and brought
high waters for you, for me a new house.

I feel your source from here:
Lake Minnetonka renewed

the way tulip bulbs push
out petals slowly from memory.

I move the sign that says *sidewalk closed*.
It will not snow today.

The gray-accented-by-green buds
will soon succumb to all green.

Thick yellow tarp stretched under the bridge,
abandoned after last year's

construction. At night, a raccoon
stares through our kitchen window

unabashed while we make snacks.
She had her babies in the hollow post

on our front porch. We'd like her
to move. The sun bears down

on my back. I feel Dorothy laughing.
I sit by the daffodil patch,

scrape wet leaves matted
at my feet with a stick. You race

along with the speed you need.
I breathe deeply. Let my body

set its own pace. A plane flies
by. A house sparrow chirps.

Steal one daffodil to press in a book.
Perhaps I'll bury her soon.

I walk against your current
under the freeway, below

the city, just far enough to still
smell its need to ingest

me whole, without thought
or desire. The beat of my feet

weaves a spell of forgiveness.
I do not care what feasts

on me. I regenerate
from memory.

Letters to Minnehaha Creek: XVII

The wind waves the tulip tree's
floppy-boned blossoms.

I stopped looking for spring
gradually, the same way I stopped

looking for Dorothy,
but today the new bouquets

on the graves decorate
for her birthday.

I remember the way forget-me-nots
border red geraniums.

Trees crochet their buds,
silently into slippers,

like expectant mothers.
Or is this

the sky smiling
with green teeth?

Her last birthday I brought
her chai from Namaste Café

that made her sick. I gave
her a Norwegian candle

that was sold at her estate sale.
The poetry books she gave me

accidently sent away to others. Warm wind
blows memories of winter from my hair.

Blue belly of a Delta plane
flies above. A willow tree

weeps small green
crescent moons,

or is that the shape
of laughter?

You speed under the sunlight
dappled on your surface.

Ice, a melted memory. Is this how it feels
to dissolve into yourself?

A layer around my heart
crumbles into its own blood.

My arms, leopard
with shadow and light.

Ants climb me,
cracks in alabaster

create a path
of dark happiness.

Grass pops out of the itchy dirt.
The black-capped chickadee cheers us on.

The trees lean as though
they whisper to you.

What do they say?
What are their green secrets?

You must find out
as the sun takes you up.

Letters to Minnehaha Creek: XVIII

This spring green,
color as precise

as belonging and fear.
My son snuggled with me

last night after a nightmare
saying, *I will hold still*

to stay with you.
Bleeding hearts are blooming.

Who would mind exchanging bare
branches for the sight of such love?

I like to think
the bubbles on your surface

kiss the sky.
Branches and leaves

rustle along your edge,
an enraptured audience applauding.

But you do not perform
for anyone. I sit on a rusty

sewer cap surrounded
by violets and crab grass.

My back to the traffic
of Minnehaha Parkway.

A shadow from a shrub
sways along my page.

I know you do not mind
living in these pages.

Everything is greening
at the speed of light.

Creeping phlox
and creeping charlie

surround the yellow
polka-dot dandelions,

a bedspread over the dirt.
Sidewalks full of tree seeds,

petals, and cut grass. Lilacs exhale
their scent past our skin.

I accept Dorothy belongs
in every living thing.

Letters to Minnehaha Creek: XIX

Lilacs shrivel and brown
quickly in this heat,

pungent scent of life
left behind.

Coral bells have not arrived yet.
Without the wind,

I could melt here.
An ugly brick back

of a bowling alley
needs a mural.

If the dandelions
will not quit,

neither will I.
Even in this heat,

I stop to touch the erect,
white bleeding hearts,

the first flower I ever loved
in my mother's garden.

Here, both
of us rippling

in the wind
is enough.

Damp scent of lily of the valley
and mowed grass.

I pass a toddler
with a black mohawk,

hand on his pop gun.
Orange poppies dangle

over the sidewalk
like melting pleasure.

Letters to Minnehaha Creek: XX

It's not your force or speed
that keeps me returning.

It's the way you separate
and drip, foam, and evaporate.

The way you operate as one
thing when you are many things.

Connected without clinging.
When those awful hands

reached in this world to carry
Dorothy away, I moaned myself hoarse.

But this world
continues as if nothing

is missing. Dorothy's family buried
her ashes at St. Mark's Cemetery

where she and I often sat
to rest. Today, I talk to her tombstone

for two hours as if her ashes
in the ground released her spirit.

The sky grays, thunder threatens,
but I keep talking.

Steal some lilies from the plant
by the Simone tomb to tuck

in the bouquet by her name.
Perhaps the dead gather in the dew

on spring mornings, hang
from petals of bleeding hearts.

Letters to Minnehaha Creek: XXI

The grapevine climbs anything,
leaves entwined in maples and oaks.

Curlicues on the shoot give it away.
I am a poet entangled with a housewife,

or maybe it is the other way around.
What gives me away?

My daughter says, *Sometimes I find
my paintings in the garbage.*

How does that happen, Mommy?
I don't know, I lie.

You are still high. A blue kayak
passes by. Last year you

were so low at this time,
the wedding anniversary

canoe ride with my husband
shifted from paddling to portaging,

frustration interlacing forgiveness.
The acupuncturist continues

to put a needle between my eyebrows.
She says, *This is your happy place.*

A lump forms and then a small bruise.
Dog tags, stroller wheels, and wind

pass over this bridge at the same time. A show
of Dorothy's hooked rugs opened.

Bright, white walls filled
with blue, red, yellow,

and green yarn climbing the space.
We all came—those who loved

and cared for her until her death. Her art:
women eating, weaving, and trampling weapons.

Poet housewife. Housewife poet.
Poem and homemaker.

Standing in the sound
of your passage, shaper

of home and poems,
mother and wife of water.

The Life of Yard Ornaments

Before the sun sets and the wild wind rests,
small plastic alligators hover
above the ground on wires that circle the small tree.

Once the sun sets and the wild wind rests,
there is no one to stop them from jumping down
to stomp and chant about the grass and the ants.

They don't care about people eating in front of TVs.
They don't care about funding cuts to the library.
They don't care about kids who placed them in the
       grass.

They may be plastic, but they still feel the chill.
They may not eat, but they still feel hunger that
       burns
and churns after the sun sets and the wild wind rests.

Summer

Letters from Minnehaha Creek: I

Squeeze the elderberry between your fingers.
Lick its juice with the curiosity of a toddler.

Follow the path into your gut;
the soft warmth of digestion, its primary work.

You know what you were built to do
in this world. You are, after all, a weeping willow.

Trunk thick and stubborn, roots spreading wide and
        deep,
strong enough to penetrate pipes.

But branches thin and supple are able
to dance with grass and kiss the moon.

Letters from Minnehaha Creek: II

Sometimes new growth is disguised as a brown leaf.
Love may sound like tires screeching at a stop sign.

Justice chases shadows. Rain loves burns.
Attend to the silent work of massaging knots from
    the soul.

Okay, might mean, *I know you are lying.*
Seasons may come all at once.

Before you were a mother, you thought everyone else
    was right.
Now you are a mother who knows some people are
    dangerous.

Apply bandages at sunset.
Unwind bandages in sunrise.

It is not necessary to always swim naked.
Dress the truth in feathers.

Letters from Minnehaha Creek: III

Sometimes a new name becomes a door
you walk through as it disappears,

absorbed into the lush woods around you.
Follow the sound of the sun

dancing on the flat-topped rock.
Some may try your old name again.

It falls from their lips slowly, a dead leaf;
its use already ended.

Make space for new leaves
to stretch toward the stars,

triangles whose points
tickle the sky green.

Afterward

I

When God cuts my poems into snowflakes
their laciness enchants me.
We string them upon the branches
of the apple tree. They rustle with the leaves.

II

I walk down the marble stairs
to the place where Dorothy is and pick
her up. She is bony and light.
The stairs go up so far I cannot see
the top. Crawling eventually, I lift her
step by step. Cold stone cannot crush me.
When I have to rest, the clouds are our bed.

III

When the apple tree flowers—white
blooms everywhere—I barely
see the poems.

IV

When I wake, Dorothy
is drinking cloud water. She strokes
my hair and kisses my cheeks,
forgives me for leaving her.
We bothknow she must walk
the rest of the way alone.

About the Author

Victoria Lin lives and writes in Minneapolis, Minnesota, and she facilitates workshops across the US. Her poems have appeared in literary journals such as *Poetry Quarterly, Paper Nautilus,* and *Apeiron Review.* She holds an M.A. in English literature from the University of St. Thomas and an M.F.A. in creative writing from Hamline University. Victoria is currently working toward a doctorate in counseling psychology at the University of St. Thomas, with plans to research and practice poetry therapy. Find her on Instagram @victoria_lin_poetry and Twitter @Victorialinph.

Publication Acknowlegments

"Alone." *Our Day's Encounter*, September 24, 2013.
"The Elm." *Northern Cardinal Review*, September 30, 2013.
"Letters to Minnehaha Creek: Prelude." *Two Hawks Quarterly*. Spring, 2014.
"Letters to Minnehaha Creek: I." *Our Day's Encounter*, September 23, 2013.
"Letters to Minnehaha Creek: II." *Linden Avenue Review*, February 2014.
"Letters to Minnehaha Creek: III." *Apeiron Review*, January, 2014.
"Letters to Minnehaha Creek: IV." *Melancholy Hyperbole*, October 5, 2013.
"Letters to Minnehaha Creek: V." *Mouse Tales Press*, January, 2014.
"Letters to Minnehaha Creek: VI." *Mouse Tales Press*, January, 2014.
"Letters to Minnehaha Creek: VII." *Poetry Quarterly*, Summer 2013.
"Letters to Minnehaha Creek: VIII." *Northern Cardinal Review*, November 29, 2013
"Letters to Minnehaha Creek: IX." *Northern Cardinal Review*, November 30, 2013.
"Letters to Minnehaha Creek: XII." *Two Hawks Quarterly*. Spring 2014.
"Letters to Minnehaha Creek: XIII." *Decades Review*, January, 2014.
"Letters to Minnehaha Creek: XIV." *Paper Nautilus*, Fall 2013

"Letters to Minnehaha Creek: XV." *Mouse Tales Press*, January, 2014.

"Letters to Minnehaha Creek: XVII." *Montucky Review*, June 3, 2013 [in manuscript now as XVIII]

"Letters to Minnehaha Creek: XIX." *Mouse Tales Press*, January, 2014.

"Letters to Minnehaha Creek: XXII," *Poppy Road Review*, April 13, 2013. [in manuscript now as XX.]

"Tracking." *Mouse Tales Press*. January, 2014.

"Walking to Meet Dorothy," *Crack the Spine*, October 2013.

All previous publications appeared under the name Victoria Peterson-Hilleque.

About the Press

Unsolicited Press is a small press in Portland, Oregon. The team publishes outstanding poetry, fiction, and creative nonfiction.

Learn more at unsolicitedpress.com.

www.ingramcontent.com/pod-product-compliance
Lightning Source LLC
Chambersburg PA
CBHW030344100526
44592CB00010B/819